GUIDE ON SPOTTING THE RIGHT NICHE ON AMAZON KDP

D1677594

JOSEPH WEALTH

COPYRIGHT

INTRODUCTION TO AMAZON KDP

Amazon KDP (Kindle Direct Publishing) is a self-publishing platform that allows authors, publishers, and content creators to easily publish their books, eBooks, audiobooks, and other digital content on the Amazon marketplace. KDP is a free service provided by Amazon that enables writers and publishers to sell their content worldwide, reaching millions of readers.

KDP was launched in 2007 and has since become one of the most popular self-publishing platforms in the world, with over a million books published using the platform. KDP allows authors to publish their books in Kindle eBook format, print-on-demand paperback format, and audiobook format through ACX (Amazon's audiobook creation exchange).

With KDP, authors have complete control over the publishing process, from formatting their manuscript to designing their book cover, setting their price, and promoting their work. The platform also provides authors with a range of tools and resources to help them create professional-looking books and reach a wider audience, including Kindle Create (a free formatting tool), Kindle Direct Publishing Select (a program that allows authors to earn more royalties and access promotional tools), and Kindle Unlimited (a subscription service that enables readers to access a wide range of books for a monthly fee).

Amazon KDP has revolutionized the publishing industry, giving writers and publishers a new way to reach readers and earn money from their work. With its easy-to-use platform and global reach, KDP has democratized the publishing process, allowing anyone with a story to tell to share their work with the world.

EXPLANATION OF AMAZON KDP

Amazon KDP, which stands for Kindle Direct Publishing, is a self-publishing platform offered by Amazon that allows authors and publishers to publish and sell their books, eBooks, and audiobooks directly to Amazon customers. It's a popular platform among independent authors and publishers who want to reach a wide audience without the need for a traditional publisher.

The platform offers various tools and services that enable authors to publish and distribute their work, set their own pricing, and earn royalties of up to 70% on sales. Additionally, KDP provides a variety of publishing options, including print-on-demand (POD) for paperback books, Kindle eBooks, and audiobooks.

Here's how the process works:

1. **Create an account:** To get started, authors and publishers can sign up for a KDP account on the platform's website. It's a straightforward process

that requires basic information such as name, address, and payment details.

2. **Prepare your manuscript:** Authors need to prepare their manuscript in a format that is compatible with Amazon's publishing guidelines. This includes formatting the text, creating a cover, and creating a Table of Contents (if applicable).

3. **Upload your manuscript:** Once the manuscript is ready, authors can upload it to KDP. The platform will automatically convert the manuscript into a Kindle eBook and make it available for sale on Amazon.

4. **Set your price:** Authors can set their own price for their eBook, and KDP provides a pricing tool that helps them calculate their royalties based on the price they set.

5. **Promote your book:** After publishing the book, authors can use various promotional tools offered by KDP to reach a wider audience. This includes running price promotions, setting up author pages, and running advertising campaigns.

6. **Track your sales:** KDP provides authors with a dashboard that allows them to track their sales in real-time. Authors can see how many copies they have sold, how much money they have earned, and other valuable data to help them improve their marketing efforts.

In addition to the above features, KDP also offers a print-on-demand (POD) service called KDP Print. This allows authors to create and sell paperback books directly through Amazon. KDP Print uses high-quality printing technology to produce books on-demand, which means that authors don't have to worry about printing and inventory costs.

Amazon KDP is a powerful platform for independent authors and publishers looking to self-publish their work. The platform offers a range of services and tools that make it easy for authors to publish and distribute their work, set their own prices, and earn royalties on sales. With KDP, authors can reach a wide audience and have the opportunity to build a successful career in self-publishing.

IMPORTANCE OF FINDING THE RIGHT NICHE ON AMAZON KDP

It can be challenging for self-published authors to stand out from the crowd and get noticed. This is where finding the right niche on Amazon KDP becomes crucial.

Here are some reasons why finding the right niche is important:

1. Targeted audience: The right niche allows you to target a specific group of readers who are interested in the type of content you are offering. This helps you to reach your target audience, and in turn, increases your chances of selling your book.

2. Reduced competition: Choosing a niche with low competition can help your book to stand out in the marketplace. It can also increase the visibility of your book, as it will be easier for readers to find it when searching for similar books.

3. Higher sales potential: When you find the right niche, you are more likely to write books that resonate with your target audience. This can lead to higher sales potential, as readers are more likely to buy books that speak to their interests and needs.

4. Better marketing: Once you have identified your niche, it becomes easier to market your book. You can use specific keywords and phrases that are relevant to your niche to optimize your book's visibility on Amazon. You can also use social media and other marketing strategies to reach your target audience.

5. Building a brand: Focusing on a niche can help you to establish yourself as an authority in your area of expertise. This can help you to build a brand and create a loyal following of readers who look forward to your next book.

Finding the right niche on Amazon KDP is essential for self-published authors who want to succeed in the competitive world of book publishing. By identifying your niche, you can target a specific group of readers, reduce competition, increase sales potential, improve marketing, and build a brand.

PURPOSE OF THE BOOK ON AMAZON KDP

The purpose of publishing a book on Amazon KDP can vary depending on the author's goals and intentions. Here are some possible purposes of publishing a book on Amazon KDP:

1. Sharing knowledge and expertise: Many authors publish books on Amazon KDP to share their knowledge and expertise with others. Whether it's a self-help book, a memoir, or a how-to guide, authors can use Amazon KDP to reach a wide audience and help people improve their lives in some way.

2. Building a brand: Amazon KDP can also be a valuable tool for building an author's brand. By publishing a book and promoting it on Amazon, social media, and other channels, authors can establish themselves as experts in their field and build a following of loyal readers.

3. Generating income: For some authors, publishing on Amazon KDP is a way to generate passive

income. By selling eBooks and paperbacks on Amazon, authors can earn royalties on each sale, which can add up over time.

4. Establishing credibility: Publishing a book on Amazon KDP can also help authors establish credibility and authority in their field. A well-written and well-researched book can demonstrate the author's expertise and help them stand out from others in their industry.

5. Fulfilling a creative ambition: Finally, publishing a book on Amazon KDP can simply be a way for authors to fulfill a creative ambition. Whether it's a novel, a collection of poetry, or a cookbook, publishing a book can be a deeply rewarding experience that allows authors to share their creativity with the world.

The purpose of publishing a book on Amazon KDP can be multifaceted and complex. From sharing knowledge and expertise to building a brand and generating income, authors can use Amazon KDP to achieve a variety of goals and reach a wide audience of readers.

HOW TO SPOT THE RIGHT NICHE ON AMAZON KDP

If you're planning to publish a book on Amazon's Kindle Direct Publishing (KDP) platform, choosing the right niche can significantly increase your chances of success. Here's a step-by-step guide on how to spot the right niche on Amazon KDP:

1. Research the market: Use Amazon's search bar to search for books in your genre. Analyze the top-selling books in your genre and take note of their category, keywords, and reviews.

2. Analyze the competition: Check out the books that are currently ranked high in your niche. Look at the book covers, titles, descriptions, and reviews. Take note of what they are doing right and what you can do better.

3. Identify the gaps: Identify the gaps in your niche that are not being fulfilled by the current books. Check out the reviews of the top-selling books and see what readers are looking for but not finding.

4. Look for trends: Keep an eye on the latest trends in your genre. Look at the books that are selling well in other formats like print and audio. You can use tools like Google Trends and Amazon Best Sellers to identify trends.

5. Consider your target audience: Identify your target audience and understand their needs and preferences. Consider factors like age, gender, interests, and buying habits.

6. Test your ideas: Use tools like Google AdWords and Facebook Ads to test your book idea. You can run ads using your book title, cover, and description to see if there is any interest in your niche.

7. Choose a profitable niche: Finally, choose a niche that has enough demand and is profitable. Look for niches that have a good balance between demand and competition.

Spotting the right niche on Amazon KDP requires thorough research and analysis. By following the above steps, you can identify a profitable niche that meets the needs and preferences of your target audience.

CONDUCTING A TOP-NOTCH RESEARCH FOR THE RIGHT NICHE ON AMAZON KDP

Conducting top-notch research for the right niche on Amazon KDP involves a combination of creativity, data analysis, and market research. Here is a detailed method for conducting research for the right niche on Amazon KDP:

1. Brainstorm Ideas: Start by brainstorming potential book ideas for your niche. Consider your own interests and expertise, as well as trends and popular topics in the market. You can also explore other platforms such as social media, blogs, and forums to find topics that are being discussed frequently.

2. Keyword Research: Conduct keyword research to identify relevant keywords and phrases that potential readers might use to search for books in

your niche. You can use free tools such as Google Keyword Planner, Ubersuggest, or Amazon's own search bar to find relevant keywords.

3. Analyze the Competition: Analyze the top-ranking books in your chosen niche to determine the competition. Look at factors such as book cover design, pricing, reviews, and book descriptions. This will help you to identify gaps in the market that you can exploit with your own book.

4. Analyze Customer Reviews: Analyze the reviews of the top-selling books in your niche to understand what readers like and dislike about the books. Pay attention to the common themes and problems that readers mention and use this information to create a better book.

5. Use Amazon's Category and Subcategory System: Amazon has a specific category and subcategory system, which helps readers to find books easily. Research the categories and subcategories in your niche, and choose the ones that are most relevant to your book.

6. Conduct a Test Launch: Before launching your book, conduct a test launch to get feedback from a small group of readers. Use this feedback to improve your book and make any necessary changes before launching it to a wider audience.

7. Optimize your Book Description: Finally, optimize your book description with relevant keywords and phrases, and make it compelling and informative to potential readers. Use your research to highlight the unique features and benefits of your book.

By following these steps, you can conduct top-notch research for the right niche on Amazon KDP and increase your chances of creating a successful book.

IMPORTANCE OF CONDUCTING RESEARCH

Conducting research is an essential aspect of learning and knowledge acquisition. It involves systematic and structured investigation to gather information and uncover new insights about a particular subject. Research plays an important role in many fields, including science, medicine, engineering, social sciences, education, business, and more. Here are some of the key reasons why conducting research is crucial:

1. Advancing knowledge: Research is the primary method through which new knowledge is created and existing knowledge is refined. It allows us to expand our understanding of the world and make new discoveries. Research helps to identify gaps in current knowledge and develop new theories and concepts to fill those gaps.

2. Developing new technologies and treatments: Research is critical in developing new technologies, medical treatments, and therapies. For example, scientific research has led to the

development of vaccines, advanced imaging technologies, and life-saving medications.

3. Solving problems: Research can help identify problems and find solutions to them. For example, research in environmental science can help identify ways to reduce pollution and protect natural resources. Research in education can help identify the best teaching methods and strategies to improve student learning.

4. Making informed decisions: Research provides the information necessary to make informed decisions. For example, research can help policymakers develop effective public policies and businesses make informed decisions about their products and services.

5. Career advancement: Conducting research is often necessary for career advancement in many fields. Professionals who are able to conduct research and produce meaningful results are highly valued in academia, government, and the private sector.

Conducting research is essential to advancing knowledge, solving problems, developing new technologies and treatments, making informed decisions, and advancing one's career. Without research, progress and innovation in all fields would be severely limited.

RESEARCHING THE CURRENT MARKET TRENDS AND BESTSELLING GENRES IN KDP

If you're an author looking to publish on KDP, it's important to understand the current market trends and bestselling genres to make informed decisions about what to write and how to market your work. Here's a step-by-step process for researching the current market trends and bestselling genres in KDP:

1. **Start with the KDP Bestseller Lists:** Amazon offers various bestseller lists on the KDP platform, such as Top 100 Paid and Top 100 Free in different genres. Analyze the books that are currently trending and see if there are any patterns or similarities in their themes, covers, descriptions, etc. You can also use tools like Publisher Rocket, KDP Rocket, or Kindlepreneur's Amazon Best Seller Calculator to extract valuable data about bestseller books in your desired genre.

2. **Analyze customer reviews:** Read through customer reviews of books in your chosen genre to

see what readers are looking for and what they appreciate in a book. You can also identify common themes, tropes, or genres that readers are attracted to.

3. **Study the competition:** Research other authors in your genre who are doing well on KDP. Look at their book covers, descriptions, and marketing strategies to identify what is working for them. Check their author bio and website to see how they connect with their readers.

4. **Conduct keyword research:** Keywords are the words and phrases that readers use to search for books on Amazon. By researching the most popular keywords in your genre, you can optimize your book's metadata (title, subtitle, description, categories, and keywords) to increase its visibility and searchability. Use Amazon's auto-suggest feature, Google's Keyword Planner, or a third-party tool like Publisher Rocket or KDP Rocket to find the most relevant keywords.

5. **Join author communities:** Joining author communities on social media or forums can give you insights into the latest trends and best practices in self-publishing. Ask questions and interact with other authors to learn from their experiences.

6. **Stay up-to-date with industry news:** Subscribe to industry newsletters, blogs, or podcasts to stay informed about the latest trends, challenges, and opportunities in the self-publishing industry. Some popular sources of information include The Creative Penn, Self-Publishing School, and The Alliance of Independent Authors.

Researching the current market trends and bestselling genres in KDP requires a combination of analytical skills, creativity, and patience. By following these steps and staying informed, you can position yourself for success as a self-published author on KDP.

UTILIZING KEYWORD RESEARCH TOOLS TO IDENTIFY POPULAR SEARCH TERMS ON KDP

Keyword research tools are an essential part of any book marketing strategy on Amazon's KDP platform. These tools help you identify popular search terms that readers use to find books similar to yours. By incorporating these popular search terms into your book's title, description, and keywords, you can improve your book's visibility and increase your chances of making sales. Here's a step-by-step process for utilizing keyword research tools to identify popular search terms on KDP:

Step 1: Identify Relevant Keywords The first step in the keyword research process is to brainstorm a list of relevant keywords for your book. These keywords should reflect the subject matter, genre, and themes of your book. For example, if you've written a romance novel set in medieval times, some relevant keywords might include "medieval romance," "historical romance," "knight in shining armor," "castle romance," and so on.

Step 2: Use Keyword Research Tools Once you've identified your list of relevant keywords, you can use keyword research tools to identify popular search terms related to those keywords. Some of the most popular keyword research tools for KDP include:

- Amazon's own search bar: As you start typing your keywords into the Amazon search bar, it will suggest popular search terms based on what other customers have searched for. You can use these suggestions to refine your list of relevant keywords and identify new ones.

- Google Keyword Planner: This is a free tool from Google that lets you enter your relevant keywords and see how often they are searched for on Google. You can use this information to identify popular search terms related to your book.

- KDP Rocket: This is a paid keyword research tool designed specifically for authors. It allows you to enter your relevant keywords and see how often they are searched for on Amazon. It also suggests other relevant keywords and provides data on how competitive each keyword is.

Step 3: Refine Your List of Keywords Once you've used these keyword research tools to identify popular search terms, you'll need to refine your list of keywords to ensure that they are relevant to your book and that you have a good mix of high- and low-competition keywords. Look for keywords that have a high search volume but low competition, as these are the keywords that will give you the best chance of ranking well on Amazon's search results.

Step 4: Incorporate Keywords into Your Book Listing once you've refined your list of keywords, you can start incorporating them into your book listing on KDP. This includes your book's title, subtitle, description, and keywords fields. Make sure that you use your most important keywords in your book's title and subtitle, as this will have the most impact on your book's visibility.

Step 5: Monitor Your Book's Performance Finally, it's important to monitor your book's performance on KDP and make adjustments to your keyword strategy as needed. Keep track of which keywords are driving the most traffic to your book and which ones are not performing as well. Use this information to adjust your keyword strategy over time and continue to optimize your book's visibility on KDP.

NARROWING DOWN THE OPTIONS ON KDP

KDP, or Kindle Direct Publishing, is a self-publishing platform operated by Amazon that allows authors to upload and sell their eBooks and paperbacks on the Amazon marketplace. When uploading a book to KDP, authors must make several decisions about their book, including its title, cover image, description, and pricing. One of the most important decisions an author must make is selecting the appropriate categories and keywords for their book.

Narrowing down the options on KDP involves choosing the most relevant and specific categories and keywords for your book. This process is important because it helps readers find your book when searching for topics related to your book's content. Here's a step-by-step guide to narrowing down the options on KDP:

1. Identify your book's main topic and subtopics: Start by identifying the main topic of your book and any subtopics that are covered in your book.

This will help you identify the most relevant categories and keywords to use.

2. Research relevant categories: Browse through the available categories on KDP to find the categories that are most relevant to your book's topic. You can use the search bar to search for specific categories or browse through the category tree to find relevant subcategories.

3. Choose the most specific categories: Once you have identified relevant categories, choose the most specific categories that accurately describe the content of your book. This will help ensure that your book appears in search results for readers who are specifically interested in your book's topic.

4. Select relevant keywords: Keywords are words or phrases that readers use to search for books on Amazon. Choose keywords that accurately describe your book's content and that readers are likely to use when searching for books on your

topic. You can use Amazon's keyword tool to find relevant keywords for your book.

5. Test and refine your categories and keywords: After you have selected your categories and keywords, it's important to test and refine them over time. Monitor your book's sales and search rankings to see if you need to adjust your categories or keywords to better reach your target audience.

By following these steps, you can narrow down the options on KDP and choose the most relevant and effective categories and keywords for your book. This will help ensure that your book reaches its intended audience and maximizes its sales potential on the Amazon marketplace.

ANALYZING THE COMPETITION IN THE CHOSEN NICHE

Analyzing the competition in a chosen niche is an essential step in developing a successful business strategy. It involves gathering information about the businesses operating in the same niche, their strengths and weaknesses, their marketing strategies, and their customer base. Here are the steps to follow when analyzing the competition in a chosen niche:

1. **Identify the key players:** The first step is to identify the businesses that operate in the chosen niche. This can be done by searching on Google, industry directories, or trade associations. You can also look for businesses that offer similar products or services and target the same customer base.

2. **Analyze their products or services:** Once you have identified the key players, the next step is to analyze their products or services. Look at their pricing, quality, and features. Identify the unique

selling points (USPs) that make them stand out from their competitors.

3. **Analyze their marketing strategies:** Look at the marketing strategies used by the key players. This can include their advertising, promotions, social media presence, and customer engagement. Identify the channels they use to reach their target audience and the messaging they use.

4. **Analyze their customer base:** Look at the customer base of the key players. Identify the demographics, psychographics, and behavior of their customers. Understand what drives their purchase decisions and what they value in a product or service.

5. **Identify their strengths and weaknesses:** Based on your analysis, identify the strengths and weaknesses of the key players. This can include their product quality, pricing, marketing strategies, customer service, and distribution channels. Understand what they do well and where they can improve.

6. **Determine your competitive advantage:** Based on your analysis, determine your competitive advantage. This is what makes your business stand out from the competition. It can be based on product quality, pricing, customer service, or any other factor that sets you apart.

7. **Develop a strategy:** Based on your analysis and competitive advantage, develop a strategy to differentiate your business from the competition. This can include pricing strategies, marketing campaigns, product innovation, or any other approach that gives you an edge.

Analyzing the competition in a chosen niche is a critical step in developing a successful business strategy. By understanding the key players, their products, marketing strategies, customer base, strengths, and weaknesses, you can develop a strategy that differentiates your business from the competition and gives you an edge in the market.

ANALYZING THE COMPETITION IN THE CHOSEN NICHE IN AMAZON KDP

Analyzing the competition in the chosen niche in Amazon KDP is an important step in the process of publishing a book. By conducting a thorough analysis of the competition, an author can determine the strengths and weaknesses of their competitors and use this information to make strategic decisions about their own book. The following are the steps involved in the process of analyzing the competition in Amazon KDP:

1. **Define the niche:** The first step in analyzing the competition is to define the niche that your book belongs to. A niche is a specific topic or genre that your book falls into. For example, if you are publishing a book about self-help, then your niche would be self-help.

2. **Conduct a keyword search:** Once you have defined your niche, conduct a keyword search on Amazon KDP to identify the top books in your niche. Keywords are the words or phrases that

people use to search for books on Amazon KDP. Use relevant keywords related to your niche to conduct the search.

3. **Analyze the top books:** Once you have identified the top books in your niche, analyze them thoroughly. Look at the title, cover design, description, and author bio. Note down the common elements that they share and the unique features that set them apart from the rest. Also, pay attention to the customer reviews and ratings to understand what readers like or dislike about the books.

4. **Identify the gaps:** Based on the analysis of the top books in your niche, identify the gaps or areas that are not covered by the existing books. This could be a topic that has not been addressed or a unique angle that has not been explored. This information can help you create a book that fills the gap and stands out in the market.

5. **Determine the pricing:** Pricing is an important factor in the success of a book. Analyze the pricing

strategy of your competitors and determine the best price for your book. You can either price your book higher or lower than the competition based on its quality, length, and other factors.

6. **Determine the marketing strategy:** Marketing is crucial for the success of any book. Based on your analysis of the competition, determine the best marketing strategy for your book. This could include social media promotions, book reviews, or email marketing campaigns.

7. **Determine the distribution strategy:** Finally, determine the distribution strategy for your book. Decide whether you want to make your book available exclusively on Amazon KDP or distribute it through other platforms as well. You can also consider offering your book in different formats, such as eBook, paperback, and audiobook, to reach a wider audience.

The competition in the chosen niche in Amazon KDP is a crucial step in the process of publishing a book. By conducting a thorough analysis of the competition, an author can make informed decisions about their book's pricing, marketing, and distribution strategies and increase their chances of success in the market.

EVALUATING THE DEMAND AND PROFITABILITY OF THE POTENTIAL NICHE IN AMAZON KDP

Evaluating the demand and profitability of a potential niche in Amazon KDP requires a thorough analysis of the market and competition.

Here are the steps to evaluate the demand and profitability of a potential niche in Amazon KDP:

1. **Brainstorm potential niches**: The first step is to brainstorm a list of potential niches that you are interested in writing about. These could be based on your personal interests, expertise, or market trends.

2. **Conduct market research:** Once you have a list of potential niches, conduct market research to determine the demand for each niche. You can use tools like Google Trends or Amazon's Best Seller Rank to see how popular each niche is.

3. **Analyze the competition:** After determining the demand for each niche, analyze the competition to

see if it's too crowded. Look at the number of books already published in the niche and their sales rank. If the competition is too high, it may be difficult to make a profit in that niche.

4. **Determine the potential profitability:** Once you have analyzed the demand and competition, estimate the potential profitability of each niche. You can use tools like KDP Rocket or Kindlepreneur's Profit Calculator to estimate how much money you can make from each book.

5. **Validate your niche:** After analyzing the market and competition, validate your niche by publishing a few books to see how they perform. You can use Amazon KDP's free publishing option to test the waters.

6. **Monitor sales and adjust accordingly:** Once you have published your books, monitor their sales and adjust your strategy accordingly. If a book is not selling well, you may need to adjust your marketing or target audience. If a niche is not profitable, consider pivoting to a different niche.

Evaluating the demand and profitability of a potential niche in Amazon KDP requires a combination of market research, competition analysis, and validation through publishing. By following these steps, you can increase your chances of success as a self-published author on Amazon KDP.

IDENTIFYING GAPS IN THE MARKET THAT CAN BE FILLED BY THE CHOSEN NICHE IN AMAZON KDP

To identify gaps in the market that can be filled by the chosen niche in Amazon KDP, there are several steps to follow:

1. **Research the competition:** The first step is to research the competition in your chosen niche. Look for books that are similar to what you want to write about and analyze their sales rank, reviews, and pricing. This will give you an idea of what is currently selling well in your niche.

2. **Identify the gaps:** Once you have analyzed the competition, identify the gaps in the market. Look

for areas where there is a high demand but little supply. For example, if you notice that there are many books on gardening, but very few on organic gardening, you could fill that gap with your book.

3. **Define your target audience:** Once you have identified the gaps in the market, define your target audience. Who is your book for? What are their interests and needs? Understanding your target audience will help you create a book that meets their specific needs.

4. **Choose your niche:** Based on your research and analysis, choose a niche that has high demand and low supply. This will give you a better chance of success and help you stand out from the competition.

5. **Create a unique angle:** To further differentiate yourself from the competition, create a unique angle for your book. This could be a new approach to an existing topic, a different perspective, or a fresh take on a popular theme.

6. **Conduct keyword research:** Conducting keyword research will help you optimize your book for Amazon search. Use tools like Google AdWords Keyword Planner or Amazon's own search bar to identify keywords that your target audience is searching for.

7. **Test your idea:** Before you start writing, test your idea with your target audience. This could be done through surveys, focus groups, or by reaching out to your target audience on social media. This will help you refine your idea and ensure that you are meeting the needs of your audience.

By following these steps, you can identify gaps in the market that can be filled by your chosen niche in Amazon KDP. This will help you create a book that meets the specific needs of your target audience and stands out from the competition.

AUDIENCE ANALYSIS IN AMAZON KDP

Audience analysis is an essential step for authors to take before publishing a book on Amazon Kindle Direct Publishing (KDP). By understanding your potential readers, you can tailor your book's content, cover design, and marketing strategies to better resonate with your target audience. Here's a step-by-step process for conducting audience analysis on Amazon KDP:

Step 1: Define Your Target Audience

The first step is to define your target audience. Who are you writing for? What age group, gender, and interests do they have? Consider their lifestyle, occupation, education, and income level. You can also analyze the audience of similar books in your genre to get a better understanding of who your target audience is.

Step 2: Conduct Keyword Research

Next, conduct keyword research on Amazon KDP. This involves finding the most relevant and popular keywords that potential readers use to search for books in your genre. Use tools like KDP Rocket or Google AdWords Keyword Planner to identify keywords that have high search volume and low competition. Incorporate these keywords into your book title, subtitle, and description to increase the visibility of your book on Amazon.

Step 3: Analyze Customer Reviews

One of the best ways to understand your target audience is to analyze customer reviews of books in your genre. Look for patterns in the reviews, such as common themes, issues, or topics that readers mention. This can help you identify what readers are looking for in books like yours and what they appreciate or dislike about similar titles.

Step 4: Create a Book Description That Appeals to Your Target Audience

Your book description should be written with your target audience in mind. Use language and phrasing that resonates with them and highlights the benefits of reading your book. Make sure to include keywords that you identified during your research.

Step 5: Optimize Your Book Cover

Your book cover is the first thing that potential readers see, so it needs to appeal to your target audience. Choose a design and color scheme that fits your genre and captures the essence of your book. Make sure your cover design is consistent with the themes and style of other popular books in your genre.

Step 6: Use Amazon Advertising

Amazon Advertising is an effective way to reach your target audience on Amazon. Use tools like Sponsored Products, Sponsored Brands, and Product Display Ads to advertise your book to customers who are likely to be interested in your genre. You can also target customers based on their interests, search terms, and previous purchases.

Conducting audience analysis is critical for authors who want to publish their books on Amazon KDP. By defining your target audience, conducting keyword research, analyzing customer reviews, creating a book description and cover that appeals to your target audience, and using Amazon Advertising, you can increase the visibility of your book and attract the right readers.

IDENTIFYING THE TARGET AUDIENCE FOR THE CHOSEN NICHE IN AMAZON KDP

Identifying the target audience is an essential step in the publishing process on Amazon Kindle Direct Publishing (KDP). By understanding the demographic and psychographic characteristics of your target audience, you can tailor your book's content, cover design, and marketing strategy to appeal to their specific needs and interests. Here's a step-by-step guide to identifying your target audience on Amazon KDP:

Step 1: Define your niche The first step is to define the niche you want to write about. This could be a genre of fiction or a non-fiction topic. For example, if you want to write a book about mindfulness, your niche would be self-help.

Step 2: Research similar books Search for books in your niche on Amazon KDP and look at their reviews and rankings. This will give you an idea of what readers are looking for and how they are responding to similar books. Read the reviews carefully to identify common themes and pain points that readers are experiencing.

Step 3: Identify your book's unique selling proposition (USP) Think about what makes your book different from other books in your niche. This could be your writing style, the tone of your book, the format, or the content itself. Identify your book's USP and how it can benefit readers.

Step 4: Identify your ideal reader Think about the demographic and psychographic characteristics of your ideal reader. This could include age, gender, income level, education level, interests, hobbies, and values. Consider what motivates them to read books in your niche and what they hope to gain from reading your book.

Step 5: Use Amazon KDP tools to research your target audience Amazon KDP provides several tools to help you research your target audience. These include:

- Amazon Author Central: Create an author profile on Amazon Author Central and use it to connect with readers. You can use the author dashboard to track book sales and reviews, and to respond to reader feedback.
- Amazon Advertising: Use Amazon Advertising to promote your book to your target audience. You can set up ads that target specific demographics, interests, and behaviors.
- KDP Select: Enroll your book in KDP Select to take advantage of promotional tools like Kindle Countdown Deals and Free Book Promotion.

These tools can help you reach a wider audience and generate more reviews.

Step 6: Tailor your book's content, cover design, and marketing strategy to your target audience Use the information you've gathered to tailor your book's content, cover design, and marketing strategy to appeal to your target audience. For example, if your target audience is young adults who are interested in self-help, you might use a modern, minimalist cover design and promote your book on social media platforms like Instagram and TikTok.

Identifying your target audience on Amazon KDP requires a combination of research and creativity. By understanding your readers' needs and interests, you can create a book that resonates with them and generates positive reviews and sales.

UNDERSTANDING THEIR DEMOGRAPHICS, INTERESTS, AND PREFERENCES IN AMAZON KDP

Understanding the demographics, interests, and preferences of potential readers is crucial to the success of any book on Amazon KDP. Here's a detailed process for understanding these factors:

1. Research your target audience: Before you start writing your book, you should research your target audience to understand their demographics, interests, and preferences. You can use tools like Google Trends, Amazon Bestsellers, and Goodreads to get insights into what readers are looking for, what genres are popular, and what topics are trending. You can also use social media platforms like Facebook, Twitter, and Instagram to gather data on your target audience's interests and preferences.

2. Define your reader personas: Once you have gathered data on your target audience, you should define your reader personas. A reader persona is a

fictional representation of your ideal reader, based on demographics, interests, and behavior. Your reader personas should include information such as age, gender, occupation, education level, hobbies, and reading preferences. This will help you tailor your book to your target audience's interests and preferences.

3. Choose the right categories and keywords: When you publish your book on Amazon KDP, you will be asked to choose categories and keywords. These categories and keywords will determine where your book appears in Amazon's search results. You should choose categories and keywords that are relevant to your book and that your target audience is likely to search for. You can use tools like KDP Rocket or Google AdWords Keyword Planner to find the best keywords.

4. Optimize your book's metadata: Your book's metadata includes its title, subtitle, description, and cover. You should optimize your metadata to make it appealing to your target audience. Your title

should be catchy and memorable, and your subtitle should convey the main benefit or value proposition of your book. Your book description should be clear and compelling, highlighting the key features and benefits of your book. Your cover should be eye-catching and professionally designed, with imagery that reflects the genre and theme of your book.

5. Leverage Amazon's marketing tools: Amazon offers several marketing tools that can help you reach your target audience, including Kindle Countdown Deals, Kindle Daily Deal, and Amazon Advertising. Kindle Countdown Deals allow you to discount your book for a limited time, while Kindle Daily Deal promotes your book to a large audience at a reduced price. Amazon Advertising allows you to target specific demographics and interests with display ads and sponsored products.

By following these steps, you can effectively understand the demographics, interests, and preferences of your target audience on Amazon KDP and tailor your book to their needs. This will increase your chances of success on the platform and help you build a loyal fan base.

ANALYZING THEIR PURCHASING BEHAVIORS AND SPENDING HABITS IN AMAZON KDP

As an author, analyzing the purchasing behaviors and spending habits of your readers can be an important aspect of understanding your audience and improving your book sales. In this article, we will outline the process of analyzing the purchasing behaviors and spending habits of readers on Amazon KDP.

Step 1: Access your sales data

The first step to analyzing purchasing behaviors and spending habits in Amazon KDP is to access your sales data. You can do this by logging in to your KDP account and navigating to the "Reports" tab. Here, you can view your sales data by date range, marketplace, and book title.

Step 2: Identify patterns in sales data

Once you have accessed your sales data, it is important to identify patterns in your sales data. This can include identifying the most popular book titles, the most popular marketplaces, and the most popular time of day or day of the week for **purchases.**

Step 3: Analyze reader reviews

Another important aspect of analyzing purchasing behaviors and spending habits on Amazon KDP is to analyze reader reviews. Reader reviews can provide valuable insight into what readers like and dislike about your book, as well as what motivates them to make a purchase. By reading through reader reviews, you may be able to identify common themes or feedback that can inform your marketing and sales strategy.

Step 4: Track marketing campaigns

Tracking the success of your marketing campaigns can also be an important aspect of analyzing purchasing behaviors and spending habits on Amazon KDP. By tracking the success of your marketing campaigns, you can identify which campaigns are most effective at driving book sales and which campaigns may need to be adjusted or discontinued.

Step 5: Utilize Amazon's data analytics tools

Amazon provides a variety of data analytics tools that can be used to analyze purchasing behaviors and spending habits on the platform. These tools include Amazon's Sales Dashboard, which provides detailed sales data by book title and marketplace, as well as Amazon's Advertising Console, which provides data on the performance of your advertising campaigns.

Step 6: Implement changes to improve book sales

Based on your analysis of purchasing behaviors and spending habits on Amazon KDP, you may need to implement changes to improve your book sales. This may include adjusting your marketing strategy, optimizing your book listing, or making changes to your book itself based on reader feedback.

Analyzing purchasing behaviors and spending habits in Amazon KDP can be an important aspect of understanding your audience and improving your book sales. By accessing your sales data, identifying patterns in your data, analyzing reader reviews, tracking marketing campaigns, utilizing Amazon's data analytics tools, and implementing changes to improve book sales, you can optimize your sales strategy and increase your book's visibility and sales on the platform.

PROCESS OF TESTING THE WATERS IN AMAZON KDP

Testing the waters in Amazon KDP refers to the process of gauging the potential of a book by allowing readers to pre-order it before its official release. This process helps authors and publishers to determine the level of interest in the book, gain early sales, and increase visibility on the Amazon platform. Here are the steps to follow when testing the waters in Amazon KDP:

1. **Prepare your book for pre-order:** To test the waters, you need to have a book that is ready for pre-order. Ensure that your book meets the requirements set by Amazon KDP, such as having a completed manuscript, a book cover, and a description of the book.

2. **Set up your pre-order:** Once your book is ready, you can set it up for pre-order on Amazon KDP. Go to your bookshelf, select the book you want to set up for pre-order, and click on "Edit eBook Details." Under the "Kindle eBook Details"

section, select "Make my book available for pre-order" and set the release date.

3. **Promote your pre-order:** After setting up your pre-order, you need to promote it to create awareness and generate interest among potential readers. You can use various marketing strategies such as social media, email marketing, and paid advertising to reach out to your audience.

4. **Analyze the pre-order data:** During the pre-order period, Amazon KDP provides authors with data on the number of pre-orders and the rank of the book on the Amazon platform. You can use this data to analyze the level of interest in your book and make informed decisions on the book's release and marketing strategy.

5. **Release your book:** Once the pre-order period is over, your book will automatically be released on the Amazon platform, and readers who pre-ordered it will receive it on their devices. Ensure that you have optimized your book's metadata, such as

keywords, categories, and description, to increase visibility and attract new readers.

6. **Monitor your book's performance:** After the book's release, you need to monitor its performance using Amazon KDP's sales dashboard. Analyze the sales data, customer reviews, and rankings to determine the book's success and identify areas for improvement.

ITesting the waters in Amazon KDP is a crucial step for authors and publishers who want to launch successful books on the Amazon platform. By following the above steps, you can gauge the potential of your book, increase its visibility, and make informed decisions on its release and marketing strategy.

PUBLISHING A FEW BOOKS IN THE CHOSEN NICHE TO TEST THE MARKET IN AMAZON KDP

Publishing books on Amazon's Kindle Direct Publishing (KDP) platform is an excellent way to test the market for your chosen niche. Here is a detailed process for publishing a few books on Amazon KDP to test the market.

1. **Choose your niche:** The first step is to choose a niche that you want to write books on. You can research what niches are popular on Amazon and pick one that interests you. Make sure to narrow down your niche to a specific topic to make your book stand out.

2. **Research your niche:** After selecting your niche, you need to research it thoroughly. Find out what the current books on your topic are, what their content is, and what makes them popular. This research will help you to understand your target audience and to write content that meets their needs.

3. **Write your book:** Once you have done your research, start writing your book. Make sure to include valuable and unique content that sets your book apart from others in your niche. You can use software like Grammarly or Hemingway to help you with grammar and sentence structure.

4. **Design your book cover:** Your book cover is the first thing that readers will see. Make sure it is eye-catching, professional-looking, and relevant to your book's content. You can use software like Canva or Adobe Photoshop to design your cover.

5. **Format your book:** Amazon KDP accepts different formats for uploading books, such as EPUB, MOBI, and PDF. You can use software like Calibre to convert your book to these formats.

6. **Upload your book:** Once your book is ready, log in to your Amazon KDP account and click on "Create a New Title." Enter your book details such as title, subtitle, author name, book description, and keywords. Upload your formatted manuscript, cover image, and any other required files.

7. **Set your price:** Amazon KDP allows you to set your book's price. You can choose between a royalty of 35% or 70%, depending on the book's price and distribution options.

8. **Launch your book:** After setting your price, preview your book and make sure everything looks good. Then, click on "Publish Your Paperback Book" or "Publish Your eBook" to launch your book on Amazon KDP.

9. **Promote your book:** Once your book is live on Amazon, it's time to promote it. You can use social media, email lists, book review sites, and other promotional tools to reach your target audience.

10. **Analyze your sales:** After your book has been live for a while, check your Amazon KDP dashboard to analyze your sales. Look for trends, analyze your readers' feedback, and adjust your marketing and promotional strategies as needed.

Publishing a few books in your chosen niche on Amazon KDP is an effective way to test the market. Follow these steps, and you will be on your way to publishing successful books on Amazon KDP.

COLLECTING AND ANALYZING DATA ON SALES, REVIEWS, AND CUSTOMER FEEDBACK IN AMAZON KDP

Collecting and analyzing data on sales, reviews, and customer feedback is an essential part of an author's success on the platform. In this article, we will go through the process of collecting and analyzing data on sales, reviews, and customer feedback in Amazon KDP.

COLLECTING DATA:

The first step in collecting data is to log in to your Amazon KDP account. Once you're in, you will have access to your book's sales data, customer reviews, and feedback. Here's how to access each of these data sources:

1. Sales Data:

To access your book's sales data, go to your KDP dashboard and click on the "Reports" tab. From there, select "Month-to-Date Unit Sales" or "Historical" reports to see your book's sales history.

2. Customer Reviews:

To access your book's customer reviews, go to your book's product page on Amazon and scroll down to the "Customer Reviews" section. Here, you can see all the reviews left by customers, including their ratings and comments.

3. Customer Feedback:

To access customer feedback, go to your KDP dashboard and click on the "Customer Feedback" tab. Here, you can see the feedback left by customers who have contacted Amazon's customer service department.

ANALYZING DATA:

Now that you've collected the data, it's time to analyze it. Here's how to do it:

1. Sales Data:

When analyzing sales data, look for patterns in your book's sales over time. For example, did sales spike after you ran a promotion or after you received a positive review? Use this information to adjust your marketing and promotional strategies.

2. Customer Reviews:

When analyzing customer reviews, look for common themes in the feedback. For example, are customers complaining about the same issue or praising the same aspect of your book? Use this information to improve your book and address any issues that customers have raised.

3. Customer Feedback:

When analyzing customer feedback, look for patterns in the types of issues customers are reporting. Use this information to address any issues that customers are experiencing and improve the customer experience.

In addition to these three data sources, you can also use Amazon's Author Central platform to analyze your book's performance. Author Central provides additional sales data, including sales by geography and sales by format (ebook or print). It also allows you to track the effectiveness of your marketing campaigns by measuring the impact on your book's sales.

Collecting and analyzing data on sales, reviews, and customer feedback is critical to an author's success on Amazon KDP. By understanding the data, authors can adjust their marketing and promotional strategies, improve their books, and enhance the customer experience, ultimately leading to increased sales and greater success on the platform.

MAKING ADJUSTMENTS TO THE NICHE, COVER DESIGNS, AND MARKETING STRATEGIES BASED ON THE RESULTS IN AMAZON KDP

One of the significant benefits of Amazon KDP is the data analytics and reporting tools that it provides to authors and publishers. These tools provide insights into sales, customer behavior, and marketing performance that can be used to make adjustments to the niche, cover designs, and marketing strategies to improve book sales. In this response, we'll take a closer look at the process of making adjustments based on Amazon KDP results.

1. **Analyze Sales Data:** The first step in making adjustments to a book's niche, cover design, or marketing strategy is to analyze the sales data in Amazon KDP. This data can give insight into the number of units sold, the number of page reads, and the royalty income generated. This information can be used to identify trends and patterns in the sales performance of the book. For example, if a book has a high number of page

reads but a low number of units sold, it could indicate that the book's cover design or marketing strategy needs improvement.

2. **Review Customer Reviews:** Amazon KDP provides a platform for readers to leave reviews and ratings for books. These reviews can provide valuable insights into the book's strengths and weaknesses. Reviews can also indicate issues with the book's niche, cover design, or marketing strategy. By analyzing the reviews, authors and publishers can gain an understanding of what readers like and dislike about the book and make adjustments accordingly.

3. **Refine Niche:** Based on the sales data and customer reviews, authors and publishers can refine the book's niche. A niche is the specific genre or category that the book falls into. For example, if the book is not selling well in the "Science Fiction" category, the author or publisher may need to consider repositioning the book in a different category, such as "Dystopian Fiction."

The key is to identify a niche that resonates with the target audience and reflects the book's content accurately.

4. **Revamp Cover Design:** The cover design is the first thing that readers see when browsing books on Amazon. Therefore, it's crucial to have a compelling cover that catches the reader's eye and entices them to click on the book. Based on the sales data and customer reviews, authors and publishers can determine if the cover design is appealing to the target audience. If not, they may need to revamp the cover design to make it more visually appealing and reflective of the book's content.

5. **Adjust Marketing Strategies:** The final step in making adjustments based on Amazon KDP results is to adjust the book's marketing strategies. Marketing strategies can include advertising, social media campaigns, book giveaways, and book reviews. By analyzing the sales data and customer reviews, authors and publishers can determine

which marketing strategies are working and which ones need improvement. For example, if the book is not selling well through advertising, the author or publisher may need to consider a different marketing approach, such as book giveaways or social media campaigns.

Making adjustments to a book's niche, cover design, and marketing strategies based on Amazon KDP results is a process of analyzing sales data, customer reviews, refining the niche, revamping the cover design, and adjusting marketing strategies. By using Amazon KDP's reporting tools, authors and publishers can gain valuable insights into their book's sales performance and make informed decisions to improve their book's chances of success.

PROMOTION AND MARKETING IN AMAZON KDP

Promotion and marketing are essential components of any successful book launch on Amazon KDP (Kindle Direct Publishing). Here are the steps involved in promoting and marketing your book on Amazon KDP:

1. **Optimize your book listing:** Your book listing should be optimized to make it attractive and easy to find. This includes a well-written book description, an attention-grabbing cover, relevant keywords, and a competitive price.

2. **Get Reviews:** Encourage your friends, family, and fans to leave reviews of your book on Amazon. These reviews can help potential buyers make a decision about purchasing your book.

3. **Leverage Amazon Advertising:** Amazon offers various advertising options to help authors promote their books. You can run ads on Amazon search results pages or on other websites that are part of the Amazon Advertising network.

4. **Use Social Media:** Social media platforms such as Facebook, Twitter, and Instagram can help you reach a wider audience. Share information about your book launch and promotions with your followers and use relevant hashtags to increase your visibility.

5. **Run promotions:** Amazon offers various promotional tools to help authors increase sales. For example, you can run a Kindle Countdown Deal, which discounts your book for a limited time to encourage sales.

6. **Participate in Amazon Programs:** Amazon has various programs that can help you promote your book. For example, you can enroll your book in Kindle Unlimited, which allows subscribers to read your book for free.

7. **Reach out to Book Bloggers and Reviewers:** There are many book bloggers and reviewers who are happy to review books in exchange for a free copy. Reach out to them and offer them a copy of your book in exchange for an honest review.

8. **Build a mailing list:** Collect email addresses from your readers and fans, and use them to promote your book launch and future releases.

Promoting and marketing your book on Amazon KDP requires a combination of tactics. By optimizing your book listing, using Amazon advertising, leveraging social media, running promotions, participating in Amazon programs, reaching out to book bloggers and reviewers, and building a mailing list, you can increase your book's visibility and sales on Amazon.

DEVELOPING A MARKETING PLAN TO PROMOTE THE BOOKS IN THE CHOSEN NICHE IN AMAZON KDP

Developing a marketing plan for promoting books in the chosen niche on Amazon KDP involves a comprehensive process that involves several steps. Here is a detailed outline of the process:

1. **Identify the target audience:** The first step in developing a marketing plan for promoting books on Amazon KDP is to identify the target audience. This involves analyzing the demographics, psychographics, and behavior of the potential readers. This information can be gathered by conducting surveys, researching online forums, and reviewing the customer data on Amazon.

2. **Set marketing objectives:** Once the target audience is identified, the next step is to set marketing objectives. These objectives should be specific, measurable, attainable, relevant, and time-bound (SMART). Examples of marketing

objectives include increasing book sales by 20% within the next six months, increasing the number of reviews by 50%, or improving the book's Amazon ranking.

3. **Conduct a competitive analysis:** Analyzing the competition is crucial in developing a marketing plan for promoting books on Amazon KDP. This involves researching the competition's books, their marketing strategies, their pricing, and their customer reviews. This information can be used to develop a unique selling proposition (USP) for the book.

4. **Develop a marketing mix:** The marketing mix is the combination of product, price, promotion, and place that will be used to promote the book on Amazon KDP. The product refers to the book itself and the features that make it unique. The price should be competitive and aligned with the book's value proposition. The promotion should be designed to reach the target audience and should include a mix of digital and traditional marketing

channels. The place refers to the platform on which the book will be sold, which is Amazon KDP.

5. **Create a content marketing plan:** Content marketing is a crucial component of promoting books on Amazon KDP. This involves creating high-quality content that is relevant and valuable to the target audience. The content can be in the form of blog posts, articles, social media posts, videos, podcasts, or infographics. The content should be optimized for search engines and should include keywords that are relevant to the target audience.

6. **Develop a social media strategy**: Social media is an effective tool for promoting books on Amazon KDP. This involves identifying the social media channels that are most relevant to the target audience and creating a strategy to engage with them. The strategy should include a mix of organic and paid social media activities, such as creating

social media posts, running social media ads, and engaging with the audience.

7. **Launch a book launch campaign:** A book launch campaign is a comprehensive marketing campaign that is designed to promote the book during its initial launch period. This involves creating buzz around the book, generating reviews, and promoting it to the target audience. The campaign should include a mix of digital and traditional marketing channels, such as email marketing, social media marketing, influencer marketing, and PR.

8. **Monitor and evaluate the marketing plan:** Finally, it is essential to monitor and evaluate the marketing plan's effectiveness regularly. This involves tracking key performance indicators (KPIs) such as book sales, customer reviews, website traffic, social media engagement, and ROI. The results should be used to refine the marketing plan continually and improve its effectiveness over time.

Developing a marketing plan for promoting books on Amazon KDP involves a comprehensive process that requires careful planning, execution, and evaluation. By following these steps, authors and publishers can develop an effective marketing plan that helps them reach their target audience, generate buzz around the book, and increase book sales on Amazon KDP.

UTILIZING VARIOUS MARKETING CHANNELS SUCH AS SOCIAL MEDIA, EMAIL MARKETING, AND PAID ADVERTISING IN PROMOTING YOUR AMAZON KDP BOOKS

Utilizing various marketing channels such as social media, email marketing, and paid advertising is crucial in promoting your Amazon KDP books. Here's a step-by-step process on how to use each channel effectively:

1. **Social Media Marketing:** Social media platforms like Facebook, Twitter, Instagram, and LinkedIn are great channels for promoting your Amazon KDP books. Here's how to use them effectively:

- Identify your target audience and choose the right social media platform where they are most active.

- Create an author page on social media platforms and share interesting content about your book, including teasers, cover reveals, and updates on your writing progress.

- Use relevant hashtags to increase visibility and reach on social media.

- Engage with your followers and respond to their comments and queries. This helps build a community of readers around your book.

- Host giveaways and contests to engage your followers and generate buzz around your book.

2. **Email Marketing:** Email marketing is a great way to reach out to your target audience directly. Here's how to use email marketing effectively:

- Build an email list of readers who are interested in your book. You can do this by offering a free sample chapter or a newsletter subscription.

- Create an email campaign that includes teasers, updates, and exclusive content about your book.
- Personalize your emails by addressing your subscribers by name and tailoring the content to their interests.
- Include a call-to-action (CTA) in your emails, such as a link to your Amazon KDP page, a discount code, or an invitation to leave a review.
- Monitor the effectiveness of your email campaigns by tracking open and click-through rates.

3. **Paid Advertising:** Paid advertising can help you reach a wider audience and increase sales for your Amazon KDP book. Here's how to use paid advertising effectively:

- Choose the right advertising platform, such as Amazon Ads, Facebook Ads, or Google AdWords.
- Define your target audience based on demographics, interests, and buying behavior.

- Set a budget for your advertising campaign and choose the right ad format, such as sponsored posts, banner ads, or search ads.
- Use eye-catching visuals and compelling copy to attract attention and generate interest in your book.
- Monitor the effectiveness of your ads by tracking click-through rates, conversion rates, and return on investment (ROI).

Promoting your Amazon KDP book requires a strategic approach that utilizes various marketing channels. By leveraging social media, email marketing, and paid advertising, you can reach a wider audience, generate buzz, and increase sales for your book.

COLLABORATING WITH INFLUENCERS AND BLOGGERS IN THE NICHE TO EXPAND THE REACH OF THE BOOKS

Collaborating with influencers and bloggers is an effective way to expand the reach of books in a particular niche. Here is a step-by-step process for collaborating with influencers and bloggers to promote books:

1. **Identify the relevant influencers and bloggers in the niche:** The first step is to identify the influencers and bloggers who have a large and engaged audience in the particular niche that the book targets. This can be done by searching for relevant keywords on social media platforms like Instagram, Twitter, and YouTube, as well as using Google to find relevant blogs.

2. **Reach out to the influencers and bloggers:** Once you have identified the relevant influencers and bloggers, the next step is to reach out to them with a personalized message. In the message, you should introduce yourself and your book, explain

why you think their audience would be interested in the book, and offer them a free copy of the book in exchange for their review or promotion.

3. **Provide influencers and bloggers with the necessary materials:** Once the influencers and bloggers agree to collaborate, you should provide them with all the necessary materials they need to promote the book. This includes the book itself, promotional images, social media posts, and any other relevant information they may need.

4. **Set clear expectations and deadlines:** To ensure that the collaboration goes smoothly, it's important to set clear expectations and deadlines with the influencers and bloggers. This includes setting a deadline for when they should post their review or promotion and specifying what exactly they should post.

5. **Monitor and track the results:** Once the collaboration is underway, it's important to monitor and track the results to see how effective it is. This includes tracking the number of clicks,

shares, and conversions that the influencers and bloggers are driving to the book.

6. **Follow up with the influencers and bloggers:** After the collaboration is over, it's important to follow up with the influencers and bloggers to thank them for their help and to see if there are any additional opportunities for collaboration in the future.

By following this process, you can effectively collaborate with influencers and bloggers to expand the reach of books in a particular niche.

IMPORTANCE OF FINDING THE RIGHT NICHE ON AMAZON KDP

With millions of books already available on Amazon, it can be challenging for new authors to get noticed and stand out from the crowd. This is where finding the right niche comes in.

A niche is a specific topic or genre that a book covers. Finding the right niche means identifying a topic that is in demand, but not oversaturated with too many similar books. It can help you target a specific audience, establish yourself as an expert in a particular area, and increase your chances of success on Amazon KDP.

Here are some reasons why finding the right niche is important for authors on Amazon KDP:

1. **Targeted audience:** When you find the right niche, you can identify your target audience and market your book directly to them. This means that you can use specific keywords, categories, and tags to reach the right readers who are interested in your topic. This can lead to more sales and better reviews, as readers who are interested in your niche are more likely to enjoy your book.

2. **Less competition:** By finding a niche that is not oversaturated, you can reduce your competition and increase your chances of standing out in the market. This means that your book is more likely

to appear on the first page of Amazon's search results, which can lead to more visibility and sales.

3. **Establish yourself as an expert:** Writing a book in a specific niche can help you establish yourself as an expert in that area. This can lead to more opportunities for speaking engagements, consulting work, and media appearances. By establishing yourself as an authority in your niche, you can also build a loyal following of readers who trust your expertise.

4. **Better royalties:** Amazon KDP offers better royalties for books that are priced between $2.99 and $9.99. By finding the right niche and targeting a specific audience, you can price your book within this range and earn a higher royalty rate. This can lead to more income for you as an author.

5. **Long-term success:** Finding the right niche can help you build a long-term career as an author. By establishing yourself as an expert in a specific area, you can build a loyal following of readers who are interested in your future work. This can

lead to more sales and success with future books, as your readers are more likely to trust and enjoy your writing.

Finding the right niche is essential for success on Amazon KDP. By identifying a specific topic or genre that is in demand, but not oversaturated, you can target a specific audience, reduce your competition, establish yourself as an expert, earn better royalties, and build a long-term career as an author.

RECAP OF THE STEPS TO SPOT THE RIGHT NICHE ON AMAZON KDP

Amazon KDP (Kindle Direct Publishing) is a popular platform for self-publishing eBooks. One of the key steps in successfully self-publishing on KDP is identifying the right niche. Here are some steps to help you spot the right niche on Amazon KDP:

1. **Research:** Start by researching different categories on Amazon. Look at the top sellers and search for books that have high sales rankings. Identify which categories have high demand but less competition.

2. **Identify your target audience:** Who are you writing for? Identify your target audience and determine what type of content they are searching for on Amazon. Think about what problems or interests they have and how your book can help them.

3. **Analyze the competition:** Look at the top-selling books in your chosen category. Analyze the titles, covers, and descriptions of these books to identify

what they have in common. Look for gaps in the market where you can offer something different.

4. **Choose a specific subcategory:** Drill down into the categories to find a more specific subcategory that aligns with your book. This will help you to reach a more targeted audience and stand out from the competition.

5. **Use keyword research:** Use tools like Google AdWords Keyword Planner or KDP Rocket to find keywords that are relevant to your book. Use these keywords in your book title, description, and metadata to increase its visibility in search results.

6. **Test your niche:** Once you have identified your niche, test it by publishing a short eBook or blog post to see if there is interest in the market. Use this feedback to refine your niche and improve your writing.

By following these steps, you can spot the right niche on Amazon KDP and increase your chances of success as a self-published author. Remember, it takes time and effort to identify the right niche, but with persistence and dedication, you can create a successful eBook that resonates with your audience.

ENCOURAGEMENT TO TAKE ACTION AND START THE JOURNEY OF SELF-PUBLISHING ON AMAZON KDP

Self-publishing on Amazon KDP can be a fulfilling and rewarding experience, but taking the first step can be daunting. Here are some encouraging reasons to help you start your journey of self-publishing on Amazon KDP.

1. **Control over your work:** When you self-publish on Amazon KDP, you retain complete control over your work. You decide how your book is formatted, edited, and marketed. You can even choose the cover design that best represents your work.

2. **Faster turnaround:** Traditional publishing can take a long time. It can take months or even years to find an agent, pitch your work, and then wait for

a publisher to take you on. With Amazon KDP, you can publish your book in just a few clicks and have it available to readers within 24 to 48 hours.

3. **No rejection letters:** Traditional publishing involves submitting your work to publishers and agents and waiting for their response. Unfortunately, rejection letters are a common occurrence, and they can be demoralizing. Self-publishing on Amazon KDP allows you to bypass this process altogether and take control of your publishing journey.

4. **Potential for greater profits:** When you self-publish on Amazon KDP, you can earn up to 70% in royalties for your e-books and up to 60% for your paperback books. This means that you have the potential to earn more money than you would through traditional publishing.

5. **Ability to reach a global audience:** Amazon KDP is available in over 100 countries, which means that your book can reach a global audience. Your book will be available on Amazon.com,

Amazon.co.uk, and other international Amazon websites, making it easy for readers to discover and purchase your work.

6. **Resources and support:** Amazon KDP provides a wealth of resources and support to help you on your publishing journey. You can access free guides, tutorials, and webinars on formatting, marketing, and promoting your book. You can also reach out to their support team for assistance with any issues you may encounter.

Self-publishing on Amazon KDP can be a fulfilling and rewarding experience. With control over your work, faster turnaround times, the potential for greater profits, and the ability to reach a global audience, it's a great opportunity to take your writing to the next level. Plus, with the resources and support available from Amazon KDP, you'll have all the tools you need to succeed. So take that first step and start your self-publishing journey today!

CONCLUSION

In conclusion, spotting the right niche is essential when it comes to publishing your book on Amazon KDP. It is not just enough to write a good book; you must also ensure that it appeals to a specific group of readers. Understanding the needs and preferences of your target audience is the key to success on Amazon KDP.

The first step to finding the right niche is to conduct thorough research on the platform. You need to analyze the categories and subcategories that are most popular on Amazon KDP and identify gaps that you can fill with your book. This will give you an idea of the kind of books that are in demand and help you identify opportunities.

Once you have identified a potential niche, the next step is to conduct in-depth research on your target audience. This includes understanding their demographics, interests, and preferences. You can use online tools and platforms such as social media and forums to gain insight into the needs of your target audience.

Another important factor to consider when selecting a niche is competition. You need to assess the level of competition in your chosen niche and identify ways to differentiate your book from others in the market. This could involve creating a unique angle or approach to your topic, offering additional value to your readers, or improving on existing books in the niche.

Finally, it is important to remember that success on Amazon KDP is not just about finding the right niche. You must also be willing to put in the work to market and promote your book to your target audience. This could involve leveraging social media, running promotions, and using advertising platforms such as Amazon Ads.

In conclusion, spotting the right niche on Amazon KDP is critical to your success as an author. By conducting thorough research, understanding your target audience, and identifying gaps in the market, you can increase your chances of success on the platform. Remember, finding the right niche is just the first step – you must also be willing to put in the effort to market and promote your book to your target audience.